DONALD TRUMP
45TH PRESIDENT OF THE UNITED STATES

BY BONNIE HINMAN

CONTENT CONSULTANT
Dr. Rachel M. Blum
Assistant Professor, Department of Political Science
Miami University

Core Library

An Imprint of Abdo Publishing
abdopublishing.com

Cover image: Donald Trump sits in the Oval Office in
the White House in the days following his election.

abdopublishing.com

Published by Abdo Publishing, a division of ABDO, PO Box 398166, Minneapolis, Minnesota 55439. Copyright © 2018 by Abdo Consulting Group, Inc. International copyrights reserved in all countries. No part of this book may be reproduced in any form without written permission from the publisher. Core Library™ is a trademark and logo of Abdo Publishing.

Printed in the United States of America, North Mankato, Minnesota
042017
092017

Cover Photo: Olivier Douliery/Sipa/AP Images
Interior Photos: Olivier Douliery/Sipa/AP Images, 1; Paul Hennessy/Alamy, 4–5; Kristin Callahan/ Everett Collection/Alamy, 7; Pictorial Press Ltd/Alamy, 10–11; iStockphoto, 16–17, 45; AP Images, 18; Kris Yeager/Shutterstock Images, 21; Shutterstock Images, 24–25; Nino Marcutti/Alamy, 27; Red Line Editorial, 28, 38; Michael Germana/Everett Collection/Alamy, 30; Rob Carr/Pool via CNP/ dpa picture alliance/Alamy, 32–33; Rick T. Wilking/AP Images, 37

Editor: Heidi Schoof
Imprint Designer: Maggie Villaume
Series Design Direction: Ryan Gale

Publisher's Cataloging-in-Publication Data

Names: Hinman, Bonnie, author.
Title: Donald Trump : 45th president of the United States / by Bonnie Hinman.
Other titles: 45th president of the United States
Description: Minneapolis, MN : Abdo Publishing, 2018. | Series: Newsmakers | Includes bibliographical references and index.
Identifiers: LCCN 2017930440 | ISBN 9781532111853 (lib. bdg.) | ISBN 9781680789706 (ebook)
Subjects: LCSH: Trump, Donald, 1946- --Juvenile literature. | Presidential candidates--United States--Biography--Juvenile literature. | Political campaigns--United States--Biography--Juvenile literature. | Presidents-- United States--Biography--Juvenile literature.
Classification: DDC 973.932 [B]--dc23
LC record available at http://lccn.loc.gov/2017930440

CONTENTS

WATCHING AND WAITING

Donald Trump stood at Trump Tower in New York City late on November 8, 2016. He was surrounded by family, business associates, political friends, and staff. They all watched the election returns on television. Indiana Governor Mike Pence was with him too. Pence was the Republican nominee for vice president. Everyone stood quietly watching the television. Trump's hands rested on his granddaughter Kai's shoulders as he stared at the screen.

The presidential campaign had been long. Much criticism had flown between Trump,

Donald Trump, *left*, and Mike Pence thank supporters at a rally after winning the 2016 presidential election.

the Republican nominee, and Hillary Clinton, the Democratic nominee. There had been name-calling and accusations from both sides. But it was over. For Trump, the campaign ended in front of a television set early on November 9, 2016.

The group would soon erupt into cheers. One by one the states announced their election totals. It soon became clear Trump had enough votes to win. He would be the 45th president of the United States.

THE TRUMP CHILDREN

Trump has five children. Donald Jr., Ivanka, and Eric work in their father's business. Their mother is Ivana Trump, who was Trump's first wife. Tiffany Trump, his second daughter, graduated in 2016 from the University of Pennsylvania. Her mother is Marla Maples, Trump's second wife. Trump's youngest child, Barron, was born in 2006. Barron's mom is Melania Trump, Trump's third wife.

AFTER THE ELECTION

The Trump family later gave a television interview about their feelings that night. Trump's son Eric said

Trump's family, *from left*, daughter Tiffany, son Donald Jr., granddaughter Kai, wife Melania, grandson Tristan, daughter Ivanka, and son Eric appeared with Trump during his campaign.

that once Pennsylvania's results were announced, the family knew Trump would win. He said that the family was high-fiving and hugging.

Trump himself remained quiet when the cheers began. He told an interviewer that the moment was amazing. He realized then that it would be a whole different life for him now.

THE VICTORY PARTY

A nearby hotel hosted the election night party. Trump, Pence, and their families arrived there at about

3:00 a.m. on November 9. They filed onto the stage in front of a wildly excited crowd. Trump told the crowd he had received a call from his opponent, Hillary Clinton. She had conceded the election to him.

It was official. Famous businessman, billionaire, and reality television star Donald Trump had sealed the biggest deal of his life. He was now President-elect Trump.

WOMAN OF FIRSTS

Trump's opponent in the 2016 election, Hillary Clinton, claimed several firsts in her political career. She was First Lady for eight years after her husband, Bill, became president in 1993. In 2000 she became the first former First Lady to be elected to public office, as a US senator. In 2009 Clinton was the first former First Lady to hold a Cabinet position. She served as secretary of state under President Barack Obama. In 2016 Clinton became the first female member of a major political party to be nominated for president.

STRAIGHT TO THE
SOURCE

In Donald Trump's election night victory speech, he talked about some of his plans for America's future:

No dream is too big, no challenge too great. Nothing we want for our future is beyond our reach. America will no longer settle for anything less than the best. We must reclaim our country's destiny and dream big and bold and daring. We have to do that. We're going to dream of things for our country, and beautiful things and successful things once again.

I want to tell the world community that while we will always put America's interests first, we will deal fairly with everyone, with everyone. All people and all other nations. We will seek common ground, not hostility; partnership, not conflict.

Source: "Full Text: Donald Trump's 2016 Election Night Victory Speech." *ABC News.* ABC News, November 9, 2016. Web. Accessed January 31, 2017.

What's the Big Idea?

Trump spoke of his dreams for America's future and for America's dealings with other countries. Write a list of key words and phrases that he used to describe America's dreams. Write a second list of key words and phrases that he used to tell how America will work with other countries.

Heyworth Public Library

GROWING UP TRUMP

Donald John Trump was born on June 14, 1946, in Queens, New York. Donald was the fourth child of Fred and Mary Anne Trump. He had two older sisters, one older brother, and one younger brother.

Donald's grandfather, Friedrich Drumpf, immigrated to the United States from Germany in 1885. He became a US citizen in 1892. The papers for his citizenship changed the spelling of his name. The family name became Trump.

Friedrich made a fortune in the Klondike gold rush in the 1890s. He traveled back to

Donald Trump graduated from the New York Military Academy in Cornwall, New York, in 1964.

Germany to find a wife. Her name was Elizabeth. She gave birth to Donald's father, Frederick, in New York City in 1905. Friedrich died during the worldwide flu epidemic in 1918. Frederick, known as Fred, became the man of the house.

THE KLONDIKE GOLD RUSH

The Klondike gold rush began in 1896. Three prospectors found gold in the Klondike River in Canada's Yukon Territory. Within a year thousands of gold seekers streamed into Canada. Many were disappointed to find that the best claims were taken. Friedrich Trump was not a gold seeker. When he arrived in the Yukon, he built a tent restaurant. Later he built a regular hotel and restaurant. He made as much money as many successful prospectors.

FRED GOES INTO BUSINESS

The Trump family lost much of its money during an economic downturn in 1920 and 1921. When Fred was 21, he went into business with his mother. They called their company Elizabeth Trump and Son. Fred built houses and gradually took on larger and larger projects. Soon he owned dozens of rental buildings. In 1936, Fred married a Scottish immigrant named Mary Anne MacLeod.

Donald Trump was born into this family of immigrants and entrepreneurs in 1946. As he grew up, he often went with his father to collect rents. Sometimes they made repairs to the rental apartments. Trump found that he loved working in business.

Donald first went to school at Kew-Forest Elementary School. He did not behave himself. He admits that he was often in trouble. He says that he once punched a music teacher. He was almost expelled in the second grade.

MILITARY SCHOOL

By the end of Donald's seventh-grade year at Kew-Forest, Fred Trump admitted defeat. He could not control Donald's behavior. Donald's parents sent him to New York Military Academy. Boys during this time sometimes went to military schools to correct their bad behavior. These schools were strict and demanding.

For Donald, the school was a turning point. He liked the uniforms and adjusted to the many rules. One teacher at the school stood out to Trump. Theodore Dobias was a World War II (1939–1945) veteran. He taught the young men that winning was everything. Donald later said Dobias was his first role model other than his father.

TRUMP THE ATHLETE

Trump's first taste of fame came while he attended New York Military Academy. The local newspaper printed a headline that read, "Trump Wins Game for NYMA." Trump had led his cadet baseball team to a victory. Trump enjoyed that brief moment of fame. He often mentions his athletic successes today.

GRADUATIONS

Donald graduated in 1964 from New York Military Academy. Next, he enrolled at Fordham University. After two years he transferred to the Wharton School of Finance at the

University of Pennsylvania. He graduated in 1968 with a degree in economics. Trump wrote later that he attended college because it was expected of him. He was not so sure he needed a degree. He already worked alongside his father. He learned about the building and rental business.

Trump worked for his father in Brooklyn for about three years after graduation. But he had bigger dreams. He wanted to build in Manhattan. He wanted to build much bigger than his father had ever done.

FURTHER EVIDENCE

Chapter Two tells about Donald Trump's life until he graduated from college and went to work for his father. Identify one of the chapter's main points. What evidence does the author provide to support this point? Read Trump's biography at the website below. Does the information presented support the main point you identified? Does it present new evidence?

DONALD TRUMP
abdocorelibrary.com/donald-trump

CHAPTER
THREE

THE BOSS

I n 1971 Trump rented a small apartment in Manhattan. He later said it was a dark and dingy place. However, Trump wanted to move up in the real estate world. He believed living in the right neighborhood was the first step. Manhattan was one of the world's most prestigious places to own property. He commuted back to Brooklyn to work in his father's office.

At about the same time, Fred made him the president of their company, Trump Management Company. Fred still worked at the business. But Trump ran it day to day. The company was later renamed the Trump Organization.

The luxurious Trump Tower on Fifth Avenue in New York City is one of the Trump Organization's key properties.

Trump, *left*, New York Mayor Ed Koch, *middle*, and New York Governor Hugh Carey, *pointing*, discuss plans for the former Commodore Hotel.

THE COMMODORE HOTEL

One of Donald Trump's first big deals in Manhattan was buying the rundown Commodore Hotel. The Commodore opened in 1919. It offered 2,000 guest rooms. It had a lobby that was the largest single room in New York City. The hotel had a telegraph room, an overseas-cable office, and a lounge. Stock prices were posted on giant boards in the lounge.

By the early 1970s the Commodore was crumbling. Competition from newer hotels had led to its decline. Trump saw the purchase price of the Commodore as a steal. Fred was not so sure. But he still lent his influence and money to help his

FOOTBALL FEVER

In 1983 Trump bought the New Jersey Generals. The Generals belonged to a new league called the United States Football League (USFL). Both the Generals and the USFL were losing money. Buying the Generals was not the kind of deal that Trump usually did. He said it was a long shot investment. He loved football. Owning a team and making it successful was a challenge he liked. Trump signed top players to the Generals. In 1986 the USFL filed a lawsuit against the National Football League (NFL). The USFL said that the NFL tried to monopolize professional football. The USFL won the case. However, it was too late. The owners voted to suspend the season. The USFL and the New Jersey Generals were finished.

THE ART OF THE DEAL

Trump's first book, *The Art of the Deal*, was published in 1987. It is part memoir and part business book. It includes 11 steps for business success. The book was written by magazine writer Tony Schwartz. Schwartz followed Trump as he went about his daily work routine. Schwartz then wrote the book from Trump's viewpoint. It was on the *New York Times* bestseller list for 51 weeks. After Trump was elected president in November 2016, *The Art of the Deal* jumped onto bestseller lists once again.

son buy the property. Trump asked for money from the New York City government. He also bargained to pay lower taxes on the building. The city agreed in order to get rid of the old building. Finally Trump was able to buy the hotel. Much of the original building was demolished. A new hotel rose in its place and opened in 1980.

Another important deal in Trump's early years was the building of Trump Tower. The 58-story building was finished in 1983. It still serves as headquarters for the Trump Organization. It also houses retail stores and condominiums.

Central Park's popular Wollman Rink is operated by the Trump Organization.

REBUILDING THE WOLLMAN RINK

In 1986 Trump took over rebuilding a famous ice-skating

rink in Central Park. Wollman Rink opened in 1950.

It closed for renovations in 1980. New York City owned it. The city thought the renovations would take two and a half years, but they were not finished by 1986. Trump offered to take over the project. He said he could complete the rink rebuilding in four months. The city refused Trump's help at first. Finally, in May 1986, it agreed to let Trump take over. Wollman Rink opened for ice skaters on November 13, 1986. Trump spent less money than budgeted.

In 1988 Trump bought the Plaza Hotel in New York City. The Plaza was a historic building. It opened in 1907 as a luxury hotel with 800 rooms. Trump had been interested in owning the Plaza for years. He admitted later that he paid more than the old hotel was worth.

PERSONAL LIFE

In April 1977 Trump married Ivana Zelnickova. Ivana was from Eastern Europe. She skied at the Olympic level as a young woman. She then became a model. The couple's first child, Donald Jr., was born later that year.

Trump put Ivana in charge of renovating the Plaza Hotel. Later she ran the hotel and some of Trump's casinos. She also gave birth to Ivanka in 1981 and Eric in 1984. The Trumps lived a luxurious lifestyle. But trouble was ahead.

EXPLORE ONLINE

Chapter Three describes some of Trump's earliest deals. The website below also focuses on Trump's business deals. As you know, every source is different. How is the information given in the website different from the information in this chapter? What information is the same? How do the two sources present information differently? What can you learn from this website?

DONALD TRUMP'S 16 BIGGEST
BUSINESS FAILURES AND SUCCESSES
abdocorelibrary.com/donald-trump

BEING DONALD TRUMP

Trump made deal after deal in the 1980s and 1990s. He was a rich man. But not all of his deals were successful. The Taj Mahal Casino was the first of his big purchases to get him in trouble. When Trump bought the casino in Atlantic City, New Jersey, it was still under construction. He borrowed a huge sum of money to finish it.

The Taj Mahal opened in 1990. But within six months of its opening, the casino was having money problems. The casino did not earn enough to make the payments on the

Trump's colorful Taj Mahal Casino lit up the boardwalk in Atlantic City, New Jersey.

loans. The Taj Mahal declared Chapter 11 corporate bankruptcy in 1991. This kind of bankruptcy filing allowed the casino to stay open. Many of the debts were wiped away. A court approved a budget and plan for Trump to repay the rest of the debts.

Two other Trump-owned Atlantic City casinos also filed for corporate bankruptcy in 1992. That same year the Plaza Hotel filed for bankruptcy as well. Trump owed too much money on the loans. The business profits were not enough to make the loan payments.

ATLANTIC CITY CASINOS

The first casino in Atlantic City, New Jersey, opened on May 26, 1978. Until then, only the state of Nevada could have gambling casinos. New Jersey voters rejected casinos in 1974. In 1976 a new proposal appeared on the ballot. Casino gambling would be allowed only in Atlantic City. This proposal passed. The Resorts International casino opened a year and a half later. Many others opened in the years following. New Jersey spends the taxes collected from the casinos on services to people with disabilities and senior citizens.

Carriages line up outside the landmark Plaza Hotel at the southern tip of Central Park in New York City.

TROUBLE AT HOME

Trump began to experience problems in his personal life too. His marriage to Ivana ended with divorce in 1992. The tabloid newspapers printed details of his personal life for many months. Trump was seeing a young woman named Marla Maples while he was still married to Ivana. Maples had moved to New York to become an actress. Trump met her in 1987. When Ivana Trump found out

TRUMP'S
INTERNATIONAL
PROPERTIES

This map shows the locations of some of Trump's properties outside the United States. Look at the map. What does it tell you about the Trump Organization? Trump has properties on all but three of the continents. One of these is Antarctica. What are the other two?

1. Trump International Hotel and Tower, Vancouver, Canada
2. Trump Ocean Club International Hotel & Tower, Panama City, Panama
3. Trump International Hotel & Tower, Toronto, Canada
4. Trump Tower, Punta del Este, Uruguay
5. Trump Towers, Istanbul, Turkey
6. Trump Tower, Baku, Azerbaijan
7. Trump International Golf Club, Dubai, United Arab Emirates
8. Trump Tower, Mumbai, India
9. Trump Towers, Pune, India
10. Trump Tower at Century City, Manila, Philippines
11. Trump World I, Seoul, South Korea

about Trump's girlfriend, she publicly told Maples to leave Trump alone. The marriage ended soon after.

Trump and Maples married in 1993. Their daughter, Tiffany, was born two months before the wedding. Trump's second marriage had troubles, too. The couple divorced in 1999.

TELEVISION STAR

Trump became a reality television star in 2004, when *The Apprentice* broadcast its first episode. Sixteen contestants competed to win a job with the Trump Organization. Teams of contestants did different projects to show their business

MAR-A-LAGO

Trump purchased the Mar-a-Lago estate in 1985. Marjorie Merriweather Post was heir to the Post cereal fortune. She built a grand estate on Florida's coast. She spared no expense to build Mar-a-Lago. The main house originally had 118 rooms, including 58 bedrooms and 33 bathrooms. Gold leaf coated the walls and ceilings. There were gold bathroom fixtures. Marble and carved stone decorated many surfaces. Post died in 1973. After Trump's election, Mar-a-Lago became a presidential retreat.

Donald Trump received a star on the Hollywood Walk of Fame for his work on *The Apprentice*. Trump's wife, Melania, and their son, Barron, joined him for the ceremony.

skills. The contestants would meet with Trump. He praised or criticized their work. In the end he would tell one unlucky contestant, "You're fired!" It became Trump's catchphrase.

Trump's two oldest children, Donald Jr. and Ivanka, joined him on *The Apprentice.* The show led to a spinoff called *Celebrity Apprentice.* Contestants were minor celebrities who competed to win money for charity.

MARRYING MELANIA

Trump married again in 2005. He had been dating Melania Knauss for several years before they married. Knauss was a fashion model from Slovenia who had immigrated to the United States. She spoke several languages. Their son, Barron, was born in 2006. Melania did some modeling after getting married, but she spent most of her time caring for Barron.

Beginning around 1999, Trump's interests began to include politics. He thought he might run for president as a third-party candidate. Earlier in his life he had declared himself a Republican and then a Democrat. Now he supported the Reform Party. Nobody could have predicted where this interest would lead.

TRUMP THE POLITICIAN

In 2000 Trump said he might campaign to be the Reform Party presidential candidate. He received a lot of negative attention from other candidates and the media. Trump dropped his campaign in the spring of 2000. He said the Reform Party was a mess.

In early 2011 Trump announced that he might run for president in 2012. He often criticized President Barack Obama. He said that Obama would not stand up to Vladimir Putin, the leader of Russia. Trump also said he was not sure Obama had been born in the

Trump has long been a political rival and critic of former president Barack Obama, who preceded him in office.

United States. This idea became known as the birther issue. Birthers had many supporters from 2008 on. Many birthers, including Trump, persisted in their belief even after Obama provided his birth certificate showing he was born in Hawaii. Trump did not end up being a candidate in 2012.

"MAKE AMERICA GREAT AGAIN"

On June 16, 2015, Trump rode an escalator down to the lobby of Trump Tower in New York City. He announced to a crowd that he was running for president in 2016. In his speech he stated that he was going to build a wall between the United States and Mexico. He said the wall would stop illegal immigrants. Building the wall was a key promise in his campaign. Trump's campaign theme became "Make America Great Again."

In July 2015, there were 17 Republican contenders for the party's presidential nomination. By May 2016, the last two of Trump's competitors, Texas senator Ted

Cruz and Ohio governor John Kasich, had dropped out of the race.

Trump accepted the Republican Party's nomination on July 21, 2016. The party convention was in Cleveland, Ohio. On July 26, the Democratic Party nominated former secretary of state Hillary Clinton to run against Trump.

THE CAMPAIGN

During the campaign, accusations flew between the two candidates. They argued about illegal immigration. Trump wanted to build a border wall. Clinton said it was expensive and unnecessary. They disagreed on who

TRUMP'S MESSAGE

Trump's message found widespread support on the campaign trail. Many people across the country felt as though they had been left behind. They lost jobs in places such as factories and coal mines. They believed that politicians did not care about their problems. But Trump said he could bring these jobs back. Supporters felt his background in business would help him make deals that would improve US industries.

should be allowed into the United States. Trump called for a ban on Muslim immigrants. Clinton said refugees from troubled parts of the world should be allowed into the country.

One of the biggest campaign issues was personal ethics. Trump faced criticism for his disrespectful comments and behavior. A leaked video from 2005 showed him making crude remarks about women. Women also came forward to accuse him of assaulting them. Trump denied the accusations.

Critics targeted Clinton, too. They said she mishandled her e-mail accounts as secretary of state. They claimed she sent important documents with an e-mail account that was not secure. The Justice Department investigated the issue. It concluded that Clinton had been careless. But it also said that there would be no charges against her.

Trump and Clinton took part in three heated debates in the months leading up to the 2016 presidential election.

THE VICTORY

Newspapers and television networks predicted a Clinton victory. However, early voting results on election night showed the opposite. Donald Trump needed 270 electoral votes to win. He received 304. Clinton won nearly 2.9 million more popular votes than Trump. But the electoral vote decides the election.

ELECTORAL AND POPULAR VOTES

The winner of a presidential election is the candidate who wins the most electoral votes. Each state has a certain number of electoral votes depending on its population. The popular vote is the number of people who voted for a particular candidate. In most states, all electoral votes are awarded to the candidate who won the popular vote in that state.

In the 2016 presidential election, Clinton won the national popular vote by nearly 2.9 million. But Trump won the electoral vote. This was possible because Trump won many more small states than Clinton. Many of Clinton's votes came from large states.

CLINTON	270 ELECTORAL	TRUMP
232	VOTES TO WIN	306

States Trump Won

States Clinton Won

ME CD 2* 1

WA 12
MT 3
ND 3
MN 10
VT 3
NH 4
ME 3
MA 11
OR 7
ID 4
SD 3
WI 10
MI 16
NY 29
RI 4
WY 3
IA 6
PA 20
CT 7
NJ 14
NV 6
UT 6
NE 5
IL 20
IN 11
OH 18
WV 5
VA 13
DE 3
CA 55
CO 9
KS 6
MO 10
KY 8
NC 15
MD 10
DC 3
AZ 11
NM 5
OK 7
AR 6
TN 11
SC 9
TX 38
MS 6
AL 9
GA 16
LA 8
AK 3
HI 4
FL 29

*Maine splits its electoral votes by Congressional districts.

Trump's victory came as a big surprise to many voters. Polls had not predicted the win. Many media members were stunned to find that they had been wrong. The next few months included many anti-Trump protests.

INAUGURATION DAY

Trump took the oath of office at his inauguration on January 20, 2017. Some groups gathered in Washington, DC, to protest Trump's election.

The ceremonies that make up the inauguration went on. Trump met with the outgoing President Obama in the morning. Then they traveled to the west side of the US Capitol building. Trump's family members and supporters watched as he recited the oath of office at noon. Now he was president of the United States. The oath ceremony was followed by lunch and a parade. Later President Trump and First Lady Melania Trump attended three balls.

INAUGURAL BALLS

The first inauguration night ball was held in 1809. First Lady Dolley Madison hosted the ball in honor of her husband James Madison's inauguration. In some years, a temporary building was built for the ball. At Ulysses S. Grant's second inauguration in 1873, the temporary building had no heat. It was freezing cold. Guests danced in their overcoats. The food was cold and the decorative canaries froze in their cages. After that the balls were held inside. Today the Presidential Inaugural Committee plans the official inaugural balls.

After the parties and formal ceremonies, it was time for President Trump to get to work. Trump said that he would make good deals for the United States. He proclaimed that he would "Make America Great Again."

STRAIGHT TO THE
SOURCE

In President Trump's inauguration address, he promised to improve the lives of the American people:

Americans want great schools for their children, safe neighborhoods for their families, and good jobs for themselves. . . . But for too many of our citizens, a different reality exists: Mothers and children trapped in poverty . . . rusted-out factories . . . an education system, flush with cash, but which leaves our young and beautiful students deprived of knowledge; and the crime and gangs and drugs that have stolen too many lives and robbed our country of so much unrealized potential. This American carnage stops right here and stops right now. We are one nation—and their pain is our pain. Their dreams are our dreams; and their success will be our success. We share one heart, one home, and one glorious destiny.

Source: Donald Trump. "The Inaugural Address." *The White House.* www.whitehouse.gov, January 20, 2017. Web. Accessed February 22, 2017.

Back It Up

In this passage Trump offers evidence to support a point. Write a paragraph describing the point he is making. Then write down two or three pieces of evidence Trump uses to make that point.

IMPORTANT
DATES

1885

Friedrich Drumpf immigrates to the United States from Germany.

1946

Donald Trump is born in Queens, New York, on June 14.

1964

Trump graduates from New York Military Academy.

1968

Trump graduates from the Wharton School at the University of Pennsylvania.

1971

Trump moves to Manhattan; he is given control of his father's business.

1977

Trump marries Ivana Zelnickova in April.

1983

Construction on Trump Tower is completed.

1993
Trump marries Marla Maples.

2004
The first episode of *The Apprentice* airs.

2005
Trump marries Melania Knauss.

2015
Trump announces a run for the presidency on June 16.

2016
Trump accepts the Republican presidential nomination on July 21.

2016
Trump is elected president of the United States on November 8.

2017
Trump is inaugurated in Washington, DC, on January 20.

STOP AND
THINK

Surprise Me

Chapter Four told about some of Trump's deals that were not successful. After reading this chapter, what two or three facts about Trump's businesses did you find surprising? Write a few sentences about each fact. Why did you find them surprising?

Take a Stand

The 2016 presidential campaign raised questions about the ethics of each candidate. Do you think personal ethics matter for politicians? Why or why not? Write a few sentences to support your opinion.

Why Do I Care?

You may not be old enough to vote, but elections and politics still affect your life. In what ways can a president's decisions affect kids? In a couple of sentences, explain how you think those decisions might affect you.

You Are There

Chapter Two tells about Trump's life at a military school. Imagine that you, too, have been sent to a military school. Write a letter to your best friend back home. Describe what you like or don't like about military school. Be sure to add some details to your letter.

GLOSSARY

accusations
crimes or wrongdoings that a person is said to have done

bankruptcy
when people or businesses legally declare that they cannot pay their debts

conceded
admitted defeat in an election

condominiums
apartments that are owned just like houses

entrepreneurs
people who start businesses and are willing to take risks to make money

ethics
standards used to measure whether something is right or wrong

immigrated
permanently moved from one country to another

memoir
a story someone writes about his or her life

monopolize
to take over something and keep competitors out unfairly

prospectors
people who look for precious metals, such as gold

renovations
changes made to an existing building

tabloid
a newspaper or magazine that focuses on gossip

LEARN
MORE

Books

Bjornlund, Lydia. *Modern Political Parties.*
    Minneapolis, MN: Abdo Publishing, 2017.

Cunningham, Kevin. *How Political Campaigns
    and Elections Work.* Minneapolis, MN: Abdo
    Publishing, 2015.

Hinman, Bonnie. *Ivanka Trump.* Minneapolis, MN: Abdo
    Publishing, 2018.

Websites

To learn more about Newsmakers, visit **abdobooklinks.com**.
These links are routinely monitored and updated to provide
the most current information available.

Visit **abdocorelibrary.com** for free additional tools for
teachers and students.

INDEX

About the Author

Bonnie Hinman has written more than 40 nonfiction books for kids. She likes to learn about all the interesting people in the news. Hinman lives in Southwest Missouri with her husband, Bill, and near her children and five grandchildren.